It's My State! ★ ★ ★ ★ ★

NORTH DAKOTA

The Peace Garden State

Doug Sanders and Ruth Bjorklund

Cavendish Square

New York

Published in 2017 by Cavendish Square Publishing, LLC
243 5th Avenue, Suite 136, New York, NY 10016

Website: cavendishsq.com

This publication represents the opinions and views of the author based on his or her personal experience, knowledge, and
research. The information in this book serves as a general guide only. The author and publisher have used their best efforts in
preparing this book and disclaim liability rising directly or indirectly from the use and application of this book.

CPSIA Compliance Information: Batch #CS16CSQ

All websites were available and accurate when this book was sent to press.

Library of Congress Cataloging-in-Publication Data

Names: Sanders, Doug, 1972- author. | Bjorklund, Ruth, author.
Title: North Dakota / Doug Sanders and Ruth Bjorklund.
Description: New York : Cavendish Square Publishing, 2016. | Series: It's my
state! | Includes index. | Description based on print version record and
CIP data provided by publisher; resource not viewed.
Identifiers: LCCN 2015051331 (print) | LCCN 2015050835 (ebook) | ISBN
9781627132527 (ebook) | ISBN 9781627132503 (library bound)
Subjects: LCSH: North Dakota--Juvenile literature.
Classification: LCC F636.3 (print) | LCC F636.3 .S363 2016 (ebook) | DDC
978.4—dc23
LC record available at http://lccn.loc.gov/2015051331

Editorial Director: David McNamara
Editor: Fletcher Doyle
Copy Editor: Nathan Heidelberger
Art Director: Jeffrey Talbot
Designer: Stephanie Flecha
Production Assistant: Karol Szymczuk
Photo Research: J8 Media

Printed in the United States of America

NORTH DAKOTA

CONTENTS

State Flower: Wild Prairie Rose

This flower has five bright pink petals arranged around a yellow center. Wild prairie roses are usually found in pastures, meadows, and beside the state's roads. They are most common in the moist and cool soils of eastern and central North Dakota.

State Bird: Western Meadowlark

Meadowlarks eat mostly spiders and insects in the summer and seeds in the winter. President Theodore Roosevelt once described the state bird as "one of our sweetest, loudest songsters ... The Plains air seems to give it voice and it will perch on top of a bush or tree and sing for hours in rich, bubbling tones."

State Insect: Convergent Lady Beetle

Convergent lady beetles, commonly called ladybugs, became the state insect in 2011 when a group of students from Kenmare Elementary School suggested the idea to an official from the state house of representatives. The convergent lady beetle's main food is a type of insect called an aphid.

NORTH DAKOTA
POPULATION: 672,591

★ State Beverage: Milk

North Dakota's legislature chose milk as the official state beverage to highlight the importance of the dairy industry. Out of North Dakota's 1.79 million cows, about 30,000 are raised for milk and produce enough milk each year to fill 1 billion glasses!

★ State Fruit: Chokecherry

The chokecherry, commonly found throughout the state, was made the state fruit in 2007. The red and black fruit of the chokecherry plant has a sour, bitter taste. It was one of the most important fruits in many Native American diets for many years, and the bark of the plant was used as a medicine.

★ State Dance: Square Dance

North Dakota's square dancers have held an annual convention for more than fifty years, usually in April. Following the instructions of the caller, groups of couples, typically four, move in rhythmic patterns, all to the sounds of a fiddle, accordion, banjo, or guitar.

The International Peace Garden marks the border with North Dakota and Manitoba, Canada.

The Peace
Garden State

About seventy million years ago, the area that includes present-day North Dakota was almost entirely covered by a shallow, warm sea. By sixty-five million years ago, the water had begun draining from the western parts of the state. A coastal plain formed in its place. The plain was made up of woodlands, marshes, and small ponds. Snails, clams, insects, fish, and amphibians clustered in the damp swampland. Predators much like today's crocodiles, reaching over 12 feet (3.6 meters) long, drifted through the waters.

By thirty million years ago, North Dakota began looking similar to how it appears today. The vast bodies of water continued to shrink and more land was added to the plains. Eventually North Dakota's four main land regions began to emerge. Many types of animals and plants thrived in the different landscapes.

The Red River Valley

The Red River forms the state's eastern border, separating North Dakota from Minnesota. The Red River valley runs along each side of this waterway. In North Dakota, the valley is a thin strip of land that stretches along the entire eastern portion of the state. Flat and fertile, the valley was once part of the floor of the ancient Lake Agassiz. The lake formed

When Lake Agassiz receded thousands of years ago, it left behind very fertile soil in the Red River valley.

at the end of the last Ice Age about ten thousand years ago. When the water eventually drained, it exposed a layer of earth rich in nutrients and deposits. This part of the state is one of the most fertile areas in the world. It is not surprising, then, that the Red River valley is one of North Dakota's main agricultural regions.

The lowest elevation in the state is in the Red River valley, near Pembina, which rises around 750 feet (229 m) above sea level. Fargo, the state's largest city, is located in this region, along with Grand Forks, another major city. Smaller towns also dot the region. Eastern North Dakota is the most populated part of the state.

North Dakota Borders

North:	Canada
South:	South Dakota
East:	Minnesota
West:	Montana

Drift Prairie

Heading west from the Red River valley, the landscape becomes more varied. Occasionally a hill gently lifts from the otherwise flat land. Here and there, a small butte, or steep outcropping, pokes out of the plains. This region is called North Dakota's Drift. In general, the Drift Prairie gains elevation along its western and southwestern edges. In the north, though, near the Pembina Hills and Turtle Mountains, the sloping land is among the steepest in the state. Some of these uplands are covered in the state's largest forests.

The Drift Prairie is known for its rich soil, made so by slow moving masses of ice, or **glaciers**, that covered it in the last Ice Age. When the glaciers slowly receded, they shrank and shifted and left behind deposits of soil, minerals, and other materials that help plants thrive. "Drift" is the name given to this rich mixture.

Those who think the plains are nothing more than flat grasslands could not be more wrong. To the west, gently rolling hills mark the horizon. Streams run at the base of shallow valleys, and many lakes dot the land. Several lakes lie in pockets carved out by glaciers. These small bodies of water are called prairie potholes. Ducks and geese stop there during their annual migrations.

The geographic center of North America is located in the Drift Prairie, near the town of Rugby in the north-central portion of the state. A 15-foot (4.5 m) -tall rock monument marks the place. Some claim that the true center of the continent is a short distance away, on private property in a farmer's field. Either way, this part of the state is approximately 1,500 miles (2,414 kilometers) from the Atlantic, Pacific, and Arctic Oceans and the Gulf of Mexico.

North Dakota's nickname, the Peace Garden State, comes from the International Peace Garden, a botanical garden on the state's northern border with Canada. The garden, which was dedicated in 1932, is a symbol of friendship between Canada and the United States.

The geographic center of the United States is marked near Rugby.

The Great Plains

The Great Plains make up almost all of southwestern North Dakota. The plains are a part of the vast plateau that runs from northern Canada to southern Texas. The portion that

NORTH DAKOTA
POPULATION BY COUNTY

County	Population	County	Population	County	Population
Adams	2,343	Grant	2,394	Ransom	5,457
Barnes	11,066	Griggs	2,420	Renville	2,470
Benson	6,660	Hettinger	2,477	Richland	16,321
Billings	783	Kidder	2,435	Rolette	13,937
Bottineau	6,429	LaMoure	4,139	Sargent	3,829
Bowman	3,151	Logan	1,990	Sheridan	1,321
Burke	1,968	McHenry	5,395	Sioux	4,153
Burleigh	81,308	McIntosh	2,809	Slope	727
Cass	149,778	McKenzie	6,360	Stark	24,199
Cavalier	3,993	McLean	8,962	Steele	1,975
Dickey	5,289	Mercer	8,424	Stutsman	21,100
Divide	2,071	Morton	27,471	Towner	2,246
Dunn	3,536	Mountrail	7,673	Traill	8,121
Eddy	2,385	Nelson	3,126	Walsh	11,119
Emmons	3,550	Oliver	1,846	Ward	61,675
Foster	3,343	Pembina	7,413	Wells	4,207
Golden Valley	1,680	Pierce	4,357	Williams	22,398
Grand Forks	66,861	Ramsey	11,451		

Source: US Bureau of the Census, 2010

The wind makes ripples in the snow on the prairie near the town of Rolla in north-central North Dakota.

Cattle find plenty to eat in the Little Missouri National Grassland in the southwestern part of the state.

includes North Dakota is called the Missouri Plateau. In North Dakota, the region begins at Couteau Slope, near the eastern bank of the Missouri River and marks a dividing point between the Drift Prairie and the Great Plains beyond. Cattle graze the hills and grasslands of the Great Plains. The area is also known for its mineral deposits, oil, and coal.

The Missouri Plateau contains the highest elevations in the state. They range from 2,000 feet (610 m) to more than 3,000 feet (914 m). North Dakota's highest point, White Butte, is found in the southwestern part of the state. White Butte is 3,506 feet (1,068 m). The state's lifeline, the Missouri River, runs through the Great Plains. When the Garrison Dam was built across the Missouri River starting in the late 1940s, Lake Sakakawea was formed. The lake stretches nearly 200 miles (322 km) to the west and has 1,340 miles (2,156 km) of shoreline. That is more shoreline than the entire coast of California.

Lake Sakakawea is named for the Shoshone/Hidatsa woman who acted as a guide and interpreter for Lewis and Clark on their expedition in 1804–1805. Many call her Sacagawea, but Native Americans in North Dakota believe her name was Sakakawea. Trees line the riverbanks in tight clusters. To the south and west of the river is a part of the plains called the Slope. This area is known for its many hills, valleys, and buttes.

The Badlands

Located in the western part of the state, the **badlands** are a thin valley made up mostly of sandstone, shale, and clay. The valley is about 190 miles (306 km) long and around 6 to 20 miles (9.6 to 32 km) wide. The Native Lakota people call the badlands "Mako Shika," or "Where the Land Breaks." Many first-time visitors are not ready for the shock and surprise that awaits them when they reach this part of North Dakota. After seeing vast stretches of gently rolling grasslands, visitors may feel as though they have suddenly entered another planet. Towering buttes, striped with layers of brown and red, twist and fold as far as the eye can see. Cone-shaped mounds and rounded domes poke up in the most unexpected places. The unusual formations of the badlands offer some of the state's most memorable scenery.

The strange shapes found in the badlands were created over millions of years. When western North Dakota was part of an inland sea seventy million years ago, layer upon layer of sediment—dirt, rock, minerals, and other natural materials—collected on the sea floor. After the water drained away, the buttes of the badlands were exposed. Their striking bands of color are the traces of each of the deposited layers. Millions of years of wind and water then sculpted the structures into the shapes seen today.

The plants, animals, and land formations of the badlands gained federal protection when the Theodore Roosevelt National Park was formed in 1947.

Bonanzaville

Fargo Air Museum

Fort Abraham Lincoln State Park

1. Audubon National Wildlife Refuge

Audubon National Wildlife Refuge is a vast stand of unspoiled grasslands and wetland habitats in Coleharbor. Named after naturalist John Audubon, the refuge is home to wildflowers and a myriad of birds, including waterfowl.

2. Bonanzaville

A re-created pioneer village in West Fargo, Bonanzaville contains forty-three historic buildings and more than four hundred thousand artifacts. Some of the buildings house museums, such as the Eugene Dahl Car Museum.

3. Cross Ranch State Park

This park lies along 7 miles (11 km) of the last undeveloped, free-flowing stretches of the Missouri River. Its 5,000 acres (2,023 hectares) feature prairies and lush river valleys. Home to abundant wildlife, it also offers recreational opportunities.

4. Fargo Air Museum

The museum houses a collection of historic aircraft, most of which are still able to fly. There are exhibits that explain the principles of flight, the history of military and local aviation, and some that are temporary and cover topics such as the Vietnam War.

5. Fort Abraham Lincoln State Park

Fort Abraham Lincoln State Park lies along the Missouri River, in the northern Great Plains. A mix of prairie, forest, shrubs, and wetlands, the park is home to a variety of wildlife, as well as historic Native American and US Cavalry encampments.

NORTH DAKOTA

6. Fort Mandan

Lewis and Clark spent the winter of 1804–1805 in Fort Mandan, which they constructed. It was there they met Sacagawea. The fort has been reconstructed, and the interpretive center, with its interactive exhibits, has been remodeled.

7. International Peace Garden

Dedicated in 1932, this 2,300-acre (931 ha) garden commemorates the peace between the United States and Canada, North American neighbors. A cairn of local stones marks the border, with flags planted on either side. Lakes, gardens, and the Peace Tower are among the features.

8. Little Missouri State Park

Little Missouri State Park includes rugged, remote badlands, called the "Little Missouri Breaks." The park is home to a variety of wildlife, including mule deer, coyotes, foxes, bobcats, and golden eagles.

9. Sully's Hill National Game Preserve

President Theodore Roosevelt set aside this national game preserve in 1904. Prairies, forests, and wetlands covering 1,674 acres (677 ha) protect numerous species of native plants and wildlife, including 250 species of birds, and a resident bison herd.

10. Theodore Roosevelt National Park

Named after President Theodore Roosevelt, North Dakota's only national park features grasslands, forests, prairies, wetlands, and badlands. Wildlife abounds, including 186 bird species, bison, wild horses, bighorn sheep, and prairie dogs.

International Peace Garden

Little Missouri State Park

Theodore Roosevelt National Park

Before he became US president and started the national park system, Theodore Roosevelt came to the area in 1883 to start a ranching operation. Struck by the area's rugged beauty, Roosevelt always held a special place in his heart for the badlands. In 1947, Theodore Roosevelt National Park was created to protect this tretch of the state. It is the only national park in North Dakota. The park covers an area of 70,447 acres (28,509 ha). More than 185 species of birds make their homes there. Roosevelt summed up the beauty of the region when he said, "The Badlands … are so fantastically broken in form and so bizarre in color as to seem hardly properly to belong to this earth."

Climate

North Dakota has what is called a continental climate. The climate is the result of North Dakota's location. That means hot summers and cold winters, little humidity, and small amounts of rain. It also means extremes in temperatures. Far from oceans, the land is not subject to the tempering effect of relatively constant ocean temperatures. Instead, the flat plains are without any natural barriers, such as tall mountains. The winds move freely across the plains. Icy blasts can cause the temperature to fall rapidly over the course of a few hours.

The average summer temperature in the northern part of the state is about 65 degrees Fahrenheit (18.3 degrees Celsius). North Dakotans living in the southern sections of the state have slightly warmer summers with average temperatures of about 70°F (21°C).

Winter temperatures average about 2°F (–16.6°C) in some parts of the state. The northeastern portion of the state tends to be colder than the southern and southwestern parts.

The amount of precipitation—rain, snow, sleet, and hail—that falls in North

Dakota changes as you move across the state. North Dakota's average snowfall is about 30 inches (76 centimeters) per year. The east usually receives more rain than the west. An average of 22 inches (56 cm) of rain falls each year in the Red River valley. Western North Dakota is drier, with parts of the region receiving less than 15 inches (38 cm) of rain per year. The most rain usually falls on North Dakota from early spring through late summer.

Summer is the ideal time to enjoy North Dakota. The amount of sunlight the state receives then is a powerful reminder of how far north it is. From mid-May through July, the state is blessed with more than fifteen hours of sunlight each day.

Wild North Dakota

North Dakota has a variety of plant and animal life. The plains are mostly treeless, so only about 1 percent of the state is covered in forest. Trees that grow in the eastern part of the state include poplar, oak, and aspen. Junipers are found on some of the state's hillsides. Cottonwood, ash, and elm trees huddle along the Missouri River Breaks. The breaks are bluffs and valleys that surround the river. From a distance, you might be able to trace the river's flow by following the rows of trees clustered on the riverbanks.

North Dakotans are treated to large areas of wild grasses and flowers that thrive on the plains. Pasque flowers, prairie mallows, purple coneflowers, black-eyed Susans, and wild prairie roses add dots of color to the green and golden grass. Together these plants provide much-needed cover and food for many of North Dakota's birds and mammals.

When driving through Theodore Roosevelt National Park, it is possible to see many different types of animals. These include mule deer, white-tailed deer, prairie dogs,

Bison herds, once a symbol of the plains, have been expanding in the state.

pronghorn antelope, bison, bighorn sheep, wild turkeys, and bull snakes. Most of these animals can also be found in other parts of the state. Patches of prairie grass often hide birds such as ring-necked pheasants, sharp-tailed grouse, and gray partridges as well as white-tailed jackrabbits, sagebrush voles, and ground squirrels.

If you walk or hike along one of the state's many trails you might hear a chorus of barks and yelps. These sounds are probably coming from prairie dogs. Large colonies of black-tailed prairie dogs are spread across North Dakota. They live in a complex maze of tunnels and dens hidden beneath the prairie.

Prairie dog towns are important to the survival of other types of animals, too. Badgers, coyotes, and long-tailed weasels prey on them. Burrowing owls, prairie rattlesnakes, cottontail rabbits, and the **endangered** black-footed ferret often take over abandoned prairie dog tunnels and dens to hide from predators or to raise their young.

Water may be precious on the plains, but fishing is still a major pastime in North Dakota. Fishers enjoy their sport all year—from a boat or from the shores of lakes, rivers, and ponds. They can even fish by drilling holes through thick layers of ice. Devils Lake, the state's largest natural body of water, is known to some people as the "Perch Capital of the World." Colorful perch thrive in the lake, along with a healthy supply of walleye, northern pike, and white bass. North Dakota has a little more than 54,000 miles (87,000 km) of river.

Ever-watchful prairie dogs are a key element of the prairie environment.

Endangered Wildlife

North Dakotans work together to try to protect their wildlife. Many laws ban the hunting of animals with small populations. Concerned citizens and government officials have also established laws and programs that protect portions of land and the plants and animals living there.

The state's bighorn sheep population is one endangered animal species that is making a comeback. Bighorn sheep were once a common sight along the Missouri and Little Missouri Rivers. By the late 1800s, though, human settlement and the increased hunting in the area reduced the population. The sheep almost completely disappeared from this part of the plains. In 1905, North Dakota's last bighorn sheep was killed near Magpie Creek, in southern McKenzie County. It was not until 1956 that efforts were made to restore the bighorn sheep population. Eighteen bighorn sheep were brought from Canada to the North Dakota badlands. They now live in nine areas in the badlands and along the Little Missouri River. In 2013, their population reached about three hundred animals. However, an outbreak of pneumonia hit the bighorn in 2015, causing many to die off. This outbreak is endangering one of the state's success stories.

Conservation efforts have increased the number of bighorn sheep in western North Dakota.

For many years, people thought that black bears and mountain lions no longer lived in the state. However, since 1990, state residents have reported seeing several mountain lions each year. Black bears have also been spotted, though it is difficult to determine how many bears live in the state. These sightings are strong signs that the state's efforts to protect its native species are working.

Bison

Black-eyed Susan

Paddlefish

1. Bighorn Sheep

Bighorn sheep live in the Little Missouri badlands. Rams' horns spiral for 35 inches (89 cm), and when fighting, rams can push with a force three times greater than their body weight. Ewes are slightly smaller.

2. Bison

Bison eat the grasses of the plains. They are one of the largest mammals in North America. The largest males weigh 2,000 pounds (907 kilograms) or more and can stand more than 6 feet (1.8 m) in height.

3. Black-Eyed Susan

Throughout the state, black-eyed Susans, with their yellow petals and black centers, are a common sight in July. The plants thrive along lower hillsides, valleys, and moist grasslands. Black-eyed Susans can grow up to 2 feet (0.6 m).

4. Jack Pine

Jack pine is a medium-sized tree. The largest in North Dakota is 48 feet tall (15 m). Most need a wildfire to force their cones open to spread seeds. Birds, squirrels, and porcupines rely on the tree for food.

5. Paddlefish

Paddlefish are dark scaled with a long, paddle-shaped snout. Many weigh more than 100 pounds (45 kg) and grow up to 7 feet (2 m). They lurk behind sandbars, dams, and slow-moving water.

6. Plains Hog-Nosed Snake

Plains hog-nosed snakes use their snouts like a shovel to burrow into the ground. Poisonous only to their prey, they eat toads, lizards, birds, and mice. When angry, they puff up and hiss, and when frightened, they dangle their tongue and play dead.

7. Prairie Falcon

Prairie falcons nest in cliffs, buttes, canyon walls, and outcroppings. They hunt squirrels, birds, lizards, and mice. They are well camouflaged, being brown with a white and brown speckled chest. They have a wing span of 40 inches (100 cm).

8. Richardson's Ground Squirrel

Richardson's ground squirrels (nicknamed flickertails) flick their tails while running. They have short ears and fuzzy tails tinged with black and are found throughout northern and eastern North Dakota.

9. Snow Goose

Millions of these swift birds (40 miles per hour or 64 kilometers per hour) migrate through the state each year. Kenmare is the snow goose capital of North Dakota, with nearly 250,000 of the birds nesting there.

10. Western Painted Turtle

These dark-shelled turtles have black and bright red and yellow undersides. They eat worms, minnows, and small wetlands plants. Western painted turtles bask in the sun on rocks and tree stumps and dive underwater when intruders are near.

Richardson's Ground Squirrel

Snow Goose

Western Painted Turtle

Fort Mandan, which was the winter home for Lewis and Clark on their journey west, has been restored. The Corps of Discovery found the original burned down.

From the Beginning

Humans first entered North Dakota about twelve thousand years ago, around the end of the last Ice Age. These people were known as the Archaic people. Most came to North America across the land bridge that once connected present-day Alaska and Siberia. That bridge disappeared below the sea when the glaciers of the Ice Age melted. Eventually the people spread across the continent, working their way south. On the plains, they hunted mammoths, mastodons, and other large mammals. The area was good for gathering foods such as nuts, berries, and plants.

From 5500 to 400 BCE, the Archaic people broke into small, **nomadic** bands. They followed the bison and sought shelter in the dry grasslands. The years between 400 BCE and 1000 CE brought another shift in their lifestyle. They continued to hunt and gather but began settling into more permanent villages. The Archaic people produced pottery and built elaborate burial mounds to honor their dead. Some of these mounds still exist and are found across the Midwest. From 1000 CE on, villages grew larger and more complex. North Dakota's Native residents built large lodges out of packed earth. They also began growing corn, beans, squash, sunflowers, and tobacco in nearby fields.

Famous artist George Catlin painted this image of a Hidatsa village along the Knife River in 1832.

When the first Europeans arrived, six main Native American groups lived in what is now North Dakota. The Arikara, Mandan, and Hidatsa settled in and near the Missouri River valley. They built lodges and farmed. During the warmer months, they headed onto the plains to hunt game such as deer and bison. When the snows came, they often set up winter camps.

The Chippewa lived in the northeastern portion of the state, while the Yankton Sioux lived near the James and Cheyenne Rivers. They were great bison hunters and became skilled riders when the horse was introduced to the region. The Lakota, or Teton Sioux, were North Dakota's most powerful Native American nation. The Lakota gained control of the southwestern part of the state and much of the plains beyond.

Early Settlers

The land that would become North Dakota changed hands several times from the 1600s to the early 1800s. In 1610, trader Henry Hudson claimed all land from Hudson Bay to eastern North Dakota for England. In 1682, René-Robert Cavelier, sieur de La Salle, who was given authority by the French king to grant and claim land, sailed down the Mississippi River and claimed all the surrounding land for France, including the Missouri River in present day North Dakota. North Dakota's official written history began in 1738 when Frenchman Pierre Gaultier de Varennes, sieur de La Vérendrye, and his sons briefly visited the area. They reached a group of Mandan villages near present-day Bismarck and wrote a series of letters about their experiences. In 1762, France gave Spain the land La Salle had claimed in North Dakota. During that time, the Seven Years' War was being fought in Europe and the French and Indian War (1754–1763) was being fought in North America. In the North American battlegrounds, Spain, France, and England fought over control of what is today Canada, the United States, and the Caribbean Islands. The Treaty of Paris, signed between the warring nations in 1763, parceled out the land, and part of what is now North Dakota was granted to Spain.

In 1800, Spain decided to give land back to France. On November 20, 1803, the land along the Missouri River had its last change of ownership. The United States made an agreement with France to buy 828,000 square miles (2,144,510 square kilometers) of land

Dogs were used by the Mandan to pull their belongings when they migrated before the arrival of horses on the plains.

The Native People

The Dakota, Lakota, and Nakota (also called the Sioux); Assiniboine; Cheyenne; Mandan; Hidatsa; and Arikara were the first Native American people of North Dakota. In the 1800s, other tribes were forced into North Dakota, including the Chippewa, Cree, Blackfeet, and Crow people.

Tribal lifestyles varied. The first inhabitants were farmers who lived in earthen homes along rivers. They grew corn, squash, and other vegetables. They made boats from trees, bark, or animal hides, and fished. They hunted deer. Other tribes were nomadic, riding horses to follow migrations of bison, deer, and elk. Needing to move quickly and with little trouble, the people lived in cone-shaped tents, or tepees, made from wood poles and animal hides.

The life of the Plains tribes changed dramatically with American expansion. The first people prospered alongside the European traders. Settlers demanded more land for farming and commerce, however, and the government obliged by obtaining Native land and selling it cheaply to homesteaders. The railroads built tracks across Native land and brought in more settlers. Countless battles were fought—many Plains tribes were warlike—and both sides suffered decades of bloodshed. In the 1870s, newcomers slaughtered the bison, killing off the Native people's source of food,

The Hidatsa lived in earthen lodges like this one, which was reconstructed near the Knife River.

shelter, and clothing. Many Native people became ill or died from European diseases, such as smallpox and measles, because their bodies had no **immunity** to foreign diseases.

By 1890, the bloodiest battles had been fought, and the United States had prevailed. The US government created **reservations**—lands set apart for the Native Americans to live on and govern themselves. Today there are five reservations in North Dakota: the Spirit

Lake Nation, home to Dakota and Lakota people; Standing Rock Nation, home to Lakota, Dakota, and Nakota people; the Three Affiliated Tribes reservation, home to the Mandan, Hidatsa, and Arikara tribes; the Turtle Mountain Band of Chippewa reservation, home to the Chippewa people; and the Lake Traverse Reservation, home to the Sisseton-Wahpeton Oyate Nation. There are more than thirty-six thousand Native Americans living in North Dakota, but there are local tribal members who live outside the state.

Spotlight on the Hidatsa

Language: The Hidatsa people spoke Hidatsa, a language related to that spoken by the Dakota. After the populations of the Hidatsa, Mandan, and Arikara were drastically reduced because of war and disease, the tribes formed a single nation. Although they spoke different languages, they learned to understand each other.

Distribution: The Hidatsa are part of the Fort Berthold Reservation of the Three Affiliated Tribes. Tribal membership is about 10,400 and 5,915 tribal members lived on the reservation as of 2014.

Housing: The Hidatsa lived in villages. Their homes were round lodges made with wooden frames and covered with packed earth. When people went hunting, they used tepees for shelter.

Clothing: Women wore long deerskin dresses and men wore breechcloths, leather leggings, and buckskin shirts. Both wore leather moccasins and in winter, long bison-hide robes. Warriors wore shirts decorated with beads, fringe, quills, and feathers. For special events, women wore dresses decorated with elk teeth and shells. Leaders sometimes wore long feathered war bonnets decorated with bison horns and fur.

Grooming: Men and women wore their hair in long braids. Both painted their faces for special events and some women had tattoos on their chins. Some men wore beards.

Food: Hidatsa women grew corn, sunflowers, beans, squash, and melons. Men fished, and they hunted deer, elk, bison, bears, and turkeys. They also ate dried bison meat called pemmican.

Crafts: Hidatsa women were noted for quillwork, embroidery, and beadwork. Men made bows and arrows, stone clubs, hatchets, spears, and knives.

for $15 million. The land included parts of present-day North Dakota and all or portions of fourteen other future states. This land deal was called the **Louisiana Purchase**.

President Thomas Jefferson was curious to know more about the land his government had just bought. He enlisted his former secretary, Captain Meriwether Lewis, to lead a group of explorers. Captain Lewis enlisted a fellow army officer, William Clark, who was accompanied by his slave, an African-American man named York, a skilled hunter and outdoorsman. The two leaders enlisted two dozen other soldiers, who together formed what is known as the Corps of Discovery. The president commissioned the corps to find a water route across the country to the Pacific Ocean. By October 1804, the corps had reached as far west as it could go along the Missouri River, in what is now North Dakota. The corps decided to build a fort, near present-day Stanton, to wait out the winter and prepare for the rest of the journey. The corps met with a council of Mandan and Hidatsa leaders who helped Lewis and Clark draw maps and gave them advice about what they might expect to encounter. In return, they offered the Mandan and Hidatsa leaders presents from the US government. The gifts included a flag, a medal bearing the image of Jefferson, the coat of a uniform, a corn mill, and a hat with a feather. Lewis wrote that the Mandans were "the most friendly, well-disposed Indians inhabiting the Missouri … brave, humane, and hospitable."

Choosing the site of Fort Mandan to winter over was a stroke of good fortune. There, they met a French fur trapper, Charbonneau, and his Native American wife, Sacagawea (spelled in North Dakota as Sakakawea). The two, with their infant child, agreed to leave with the corps in the spring and act as guides and interpreters. The corps left Fort Mandan in April 1805. As they made their way west to what is now Oregon and Washington, the presence of Sacagawea and her child smoothed the way for the corps in their many meetings with other Native tribes. In 1806, on their return trip, the corps passed through Mandan territory again and were surprised and dismayed to find that their fort had burned down.

Early Settlers

Lewis and Clark's journey was an important step in settling the region. Beginning in the 1790s, fur trappers and traders established trade routes from the Great Lakes to the Native villages along the Missouri River in North Dakota. Over the next century, people from far-off places would make their way to North Dakota. Europeans moved to the area to trap and trade for furs. Many set up trading posts. Some of the first were set up along the Knife River, to trade with the Mandan and Hidatsa villagers. Others were set up at Pembina, Park River, the Missouri River, and Grand Forks. In 1801, Alexander Henry established a trading post in Pembina. In 1812, Scottish and Irish families from Canada built the state's first settlement there. That settlement at Pembina and a fur trading post in Walhalla are, other than the original thirteen colonies, among the oldest communities in the nation. From the mid-1700s, the French and British competed for control of the fur trade with the Native Americans. Later, the Spanish tried without success to get their share of the profits. After the Louisiana Purchase, control of the fur trade slowly tipped to the American side. By the mid-nineteenth century, fur companies had built trading posts along the Mississippi River valley and driven out British trappers and traders. From 1828 to 1867,

Artist Karl Bodmer painted the Fort Union Trading Post, where goods were bought and swapped.

Making a Winter Count

Many Native people recorded the events of the year on an animal hide, some on buffalo robes. Events included animals hunted, fish caught, bows and arrows made, plants grown or foraged, villages set up, and people they met.

What You Need

Sheet of brown kraft paper or paper shopping bag

Bucket of water

Watercolor paintbrushes

Assorted colors of watercolors

Brown powdered tempera paint

Rubber gloves

Hair dryer (optional)

A few sheets of newspaper

What To Do

- Tear paper (do not cut—you want a jagged edge) into the shape of an animal: bear, wolf, bison, or raccoon.
- Crumple the sheet of paper into a ball.
- Mix brown powdered tempera paint into bucket of water.
- Wearing gloves, put rumpled paper in bucket and "knead" gently.
- Set out newspaper.
- Flatten and lay brown paper "hide" on newspaper to dry. Carefully use a hair dryer if you choose.
- Once dry, paint your "year" in a circle or spiral shape on the "hide." Some suggestions: birthday presents, holiday symbols, pets, family, friends, vacations, and home. Or choose to paint Native American symbols: tepees, bows and arrows, bears, wolves, deer, elk, rabbits, bison, turkeys, mountains, rivers, the sun, the moon, and more.

the Fort Union Trading Post was the main fur-trading station in the Upper Missouri River region. The success of trading in the region led to better transportation routes. More settlements also sprang up along the plains.

Scientific Discoveries

Following in the footsteps of the Corps of Discovery, there were other adventurers who were not interested in the fur trade but were instead on scientific and fact-finding expeditions. In 1811, John Bradbury and Thomas Nuttel left the comfort of Philadelphia and embarked on a journey up the Missouri River and then out to Oregon. Their mission was to collect plant specimens that were unknown to Europeans. In 1833, a German prince and **naturalist**, Maximillian of Weid, explored the area with Swiss artist Karl Bodmer. Bodmer painted portraits of famous Native American chiefs, as well as landscapes. Later, mapmakers Joseph Nicollette and John C. Frémont passed through on their way west and drew maps of the Upper Missouri River region. In 1843, naturalist John Audubon, known for his famous work studying and drawing the birds of North America, traveled up the Missouri River in search of new species of mammals. His final stop in North Dakota was at Fort Union, where he described several before unknown species. The last bird that he discovered was a North Dakota native, the Baird's sparrow.

Sitting Bull, the chief of the Lakota, was killed in 1890.

The "Indian Wars"

The discovery of gold in California and Montana in the 1840s and 1850s brought even more traffic to the state. Pioneers heading west began to blaze their trails through traditional Native American lands.

North Dakota's Native Americans were not pleased with the arrival of these newcomers. For years, the fur trade had been good for both Native Americans and Europeans. The peace and calm were about to end, though. As more newcomers entered the region, the Native American way of life changed for the worse.

North Dakota had been part of the Minnesota Territory, but Minnesota became a state in 1858, so governance of North Dakota was left to the military until 1861, when the Dakota Territory was established. Clashes between the Native people and the newcomers grew increasingly violent. Starvation, broken treaties, and loss of land led to the Minnesota Uprising in 1862, when hundreds of Minnesota settlers were killed by Lakota warriors who then fled into North Dakota. The government sent more than four thousand troops under generals Alfred Sully and Henry Hastings Sibley to capture them. On September 3, 1863, the US forces defeated the Native fighters at the Battle of Whitestone Hill and went on to destroy other Native American encampments in the area. In 1864, Sully's troops attacked a large camp of Native Americans in the Killdeer Mountains, driving them west into the badlands. Sully's men gave chase but soon became lost in the badlands' twists and turns. Although the Native Americans escaped that assault, the attacks continued. Another major campaign was launched in 1865. The government's plan to push the Native Americans farther west was working. Though small **skirmishes** continued, North Dakota's Native Americans were mostly defeated. Peace finally arrived in 1881, when the great leader Chief Sitting Bull surrendered. Afterward, many Native Americans were required to live on reservations.

"A Delightsome Land"

The Dakota Territory was named for the Lakota word meaning "friends" or "allies." The territory included all of present-day North and South Dakota and large parts of Wyoming and Montana. In 1863, the territory was opened to settlers who wanted to farm the land. Called homesteaders, they were offered free patches of land if they lived on it and worked it for a given number of years. The government expected several thousands to accept the offer, but only a small trickle of people flowed into the state. They came by wagon, steamboat, and stagecoach.

Many settlers thought that the region was too far from everything. Most pioneers headed to places that were not quite so remote or to places farther west. By the early 1870s, only about thirty families had officially registered their land claims. Territory officials needed to find a way to draw more people to the Dakota Territory.

A work gang putting down tracks for the St. Paul, Minneapolis, and Manitoba Railway Company was photographed in the late 1880s west of Minot.

In the 1870s and 1880s, the railroads and the government joined forces. They took out advertisements that promoted settlement in the Dakota Territory. The ads called the Dakotas "a delightsome land," where free—or cheap—land awaited them, "ready for the plow." The Northern Pacific Railroad started laying track across northern parts of the state in 1872. Slowly the population started to grow.

By the late 1870s, large farming operations were established in the state. Families and companies from the East set up huge wheat farms. The farms ranged from 3,000 to 65,000 acres (1,214 to 26,305 ha) and were mostly found in the Red River valley. They were so successful and earned such large profits that they were called bonanza farms. Ranching also became popular in the region. Cattle companies spread into the badlands. Future US president Theodore Roosevelt helped open up land for ranching along the Little Missouri River. By 1889, more than 2,000 miles (3,219 km) of railroad tracks crisscrossed the state. The region was finally prepared to join the Union. On November 2, 1889, North Dakota officially became a state.

10 KEY CITIES ★ ★ ★

Grand Forks

Minot

1. Fargo: population 105,549

Fargo lies on the Red River and is the state's largest city, home to universities and colleges, theaters, symphonies, museums, hospitals, factories, and businesses. People flock to the Fargodome—a venue for major concerts, sporting events, traveling cultural performances, art fairs, and festivals.

2. Bismarck: population 61,272

Bismarck, the state capital, was founded in 1872 and named for German leader Otto von Bismarck. State promoters hoped the name would encourage German farmers to settle there. Bismarck first boomed when gold was discovered in the nearby Black Hills.

3. Grand Forks: population 52,838

Grand Forks lies at the fork of the Red and Red Lake Rivers and was historically an important trading center. The city grew when a US Air Force base was established nearby. It is home to the University of North Dakota.

4. Minot: population 40,888

Minot, once a trading post, thrives today. Rich farmland along the Missouri River, as well as the nearby Minot Air Force Base and the Bakken oil fields, make Minot home to farmers, oil workers, and military personnel.

5. West Fargo: population 25,830

West Fargo was founded in 1926 and is one of the state's fastest growing cities. Tree-lined streets, good public schools, shopping centers, and city parks make the city a popular suburban community.

6. Mandan: population 18,331

Mandan is located across the Missouri River from Bismarck. Being situated in a historic location, Mandan is near Fort Abraham Lincoln State Park, restored frontier US Army forts, and the ruins of a Mandan village

7. Dickinson: population 17,787

Dickinson is home to Dickinson State University and the Dakota Dinosaur Museum (*right*). It is the center of commerce for southwestern North Dakota and is close to the state's largest **reservoir**, Lake Sakakawea.

8. Jamestown: population 15,427

Jamestown lies along the James River and three reservoirs, popular for recreation. The city is also home to a school for disabled children, one of the country's leading such schools. Jamestown was the first city in the nation to install wheelchair sidewalk cutouts.

9. Williston: population 14,716

Williston, near the **confluence** of the Missouri and Yellowstone Rivers, was a farming town but now bursts at the seams with oil field workers. Williston's population has doubled since the 2010 census, which makes it unofficially the state's fifth largest city.

10. Wahpeton: population 7,766

Wahpeton lies along the Red River and first grew as a boatbuilding town for commercial riverboats. When the railroad replaced river traffic, the townspeople, settlers from Germany and Scandinavia, began farming the valley.

Dickinson

Williston

Lacking trees to make homes on the prairies, settlers built with sod.

By the 1890s, the boom was over. Not as many people moved into the state. Wheat prices started to fall. Many of the large bonanza farms were divided into smaller properties. The state's residents continued to make money, but on a smaller scale. Still, North Dakota continued to grow. Coal mining was introduced to the region. Newcomers still came to claim the available land. Many arrived from faraway places, and the region slowly became a blend of cultures. Most of the state's new residents came from Norway, Germany, and Russia. Great numbers also arrived from Finland, Canada, Denmark, England, Ireland, Sweden, Hungary, Scotland, and Austria. A group of farmers from Iceland settled near the Pembina **Escarpment**, a rocky hill region that reminded them of home.

Life was often hard for these settlers trying to squeeze a living out of the land. To claim their land, residents had to build at least a one-room home on their property. However, wood was scarce

Bonza Bonanza

In 1802, Pierre Bonza and his wife became the parents of the first non-Native American child born in North Dakota. The couple were African Americans who had been enslaved. Pierre Bonza worked as an interpreter for the Northwest Fur Company on the Red River.

on the mostly treeless northern plains. Some families ordered lumber and hauled it for miles from the closest railroad station. Unfortunately, few could afford such a luxury. The settlers were forced to be creative. They looked to the land for an answer. Some scooped large holes out of the banks of streams. These homes were called **dugouts**. Most settlers chose to build with sod. This was the top layer of soil, which was held firmly together by the roots of the grasses. Settlers cut great chunks of sod out of the prairie and shaped it into blocks. The blocks were stacked to form simple homes. Sod proved to be a good building material. It was inexpensive and fairly sturdy. Sometimes wind, rain, and small animals forced their way through the cracks and seams in these sod houses, though. Some German and Russian settlers began building homes made of bricks of sun-dried mud. Eventually, many pioneer families made their homes out of this material.

Debut Voyage

Wealthy businessman John Jacob Astor commissioned the first steam-powered boats for travel on the Mississippi and Missouri Rivers. The first, named the *Yellowstone*, reached its destination, Fort Union, in June 1832, to fur traders' and Native Americans' astonishment.

A Call for Change

Starting in the 1880s, North Dakota's farmers were faced with new challenges. Fighting drought and harsh weather was hard enough, but now the railroads added to their problems. Some North Dakotans felt that the railroad companies had too much control. The farmers needed the railroads to ship their products to markets in the East. However, the railroads often charged high prices for their services. Few farmers could afford these expenses. In 1884, a group of farmers formed the Dakota Farmers' Alliance (DFA). Within four years, the group had twenty-eight thousand members. Together they built grain elevators and warehouses to store their crops. They also started a group to buy coal and supplies. Combining their goods and money made it easier to ship and sell their goods. They also published a magazine called *Dakota Farmer*. The alliance slowly gained power and popularity. By 1892, the DFA had strong political power in the state legislature.

Groups such as the DFA were formed not just to fight the railroads. Other organizations worked together to fight political "bosses." These were powerful and wealthy business leaders who controlled much of the state. By the 1890s, "Boss" Alexander McKenzie had a tight grip on North Dakota politics. He bribed officials in order to create

Trains, such as this one making a stop in the Dakota Territory, reduced travel time for settlers.

the state lottery. He controlled the selection of state senators in 1893. Concerned citizens wanted to end this imbalance of power and to lessen the bosses' control.

Change came in the first decade of the 1900s. A spirit of reform was slowly gripping the state. In 1907, Democratic governor John Burke took office and called for sweeping changes. He passed a series of laws aimed at railroad reform, child labor protection, workers' compensation, and food and drug purity. Students benefited from the reforms as well. Education improved as the state began training more qualified teachers. Soon one-room schoolhouses were established in places where no schools had existed before. More colleges opened their doors for the first time in the state.

From the late 1890s to the mid-1910s, North Dakota experienced another boom. Better farm machinery and more effective farming methods were two of the driving forces. About twenty-five thousand new residents—still mostly Europeans—arrived during this period. By the 1910s, the control of the political bosses had ended. Farmers continued to look for ways to make their lives easier. In 1915, they formed the Nonpartisan League. Within a year, forty thousand farmers had joined. The group believed the state should own grain-processing centers, shipping centers, and storage areas. It also called for banks that would grant farmers low-interest loans to be set up in agricultural areas.

Tough Times

In the 1920s, hard times hit the state once again. Weather patterns changed, and a series of droughts gripped most of North Dakota. Dust storms raged in the western part of the state, which only added to the problems. Throughout the 1920s and 1930s, there was little rain. Grasshoppers descended on the land, destroying crops. The price of grain also dropped. To make matters worse, diseases such as stem rust infected much of the state's wheat crop.

In 1929, the United States was faced with the **Great Depression**. Across the country people lost their jobs and could not find ways to support their families. Farmers began

The Great Depression caused great suffering in the towns and on the farms of North Dakota.

Good Out of Suffering

In 1884, after the deaths of his mother and wife, Theodore Roosevelt sought comfort in a cabin in North Dakota's badlands. Later, when president, his wilderness experience led him to create 150 national forests, 23 national parks and monuments, and many wildlife refuges.

to suffer, too. Because of the weak economy, few people could afford to buy farm produce. In North Dakota, many families lost their homes. Banks foreclosed on, or took away, their homesteads. Before long, even the banks began to fail and were forced to close. By 1933, more than half of North Dakota's banks had failed. Of the 898 that existed in the state in 1920, only 343 remained.

Some relief came in the form of a series of programs run by the US government. The Works Progress Administration (WPA) hired people to build highways, wells, and irrigation systems, sewage-treatment plants, schools, and recreation sites across the state. There were three Civilian Conservation Corps (CCC) camps stationed in North Dakota from 1934 to 1941. The CCCs worked building structures for parks, such as Turtle River State Park, Chateau de Mores State Historic Site, and Devil's Lake. Projects such as these provided much-needed jobs for North Dakotans. Historian Elwyn B. Robinson wrote that during the 1930s, relief was "the biggest business in the state."

World War II also helped the state's economy recover. North Dakota supplied food and other goods to the troops. In the early 1940s, the state's fields and farms were producing more grain than ever before. This created surpluses, or too much grain. As a result, the prices of these crops started to fall again. It was another shift the state was forced to face. In the last half of the twentieth century, fewer farms dotted the North Dakota landscape. Machines replaced workers in the fields. People started moving to the cities and larger towns in search of jobs.

Into the Future

In the last half of the twentieth century, North Dakota continued to grow and change. Officials needed to create new

In Their Own Words

"Wild beasts and birds are by right not the property merely of the people who are alive today, but the property of unknown generations, whose belongings we have no right to squander."
—President Theodore Roosevelt, 1903, in establishing national wildlife refuges

Flooding in 2011 forced many people to evacuate their homes.

jobs and industries and, at the same time, protect the state's environment and resources. In 1968, the Garrison Diversion Project began. It included a system of canals that channeled water from the Missouri River to the state's farmland. The system was also designed to supply water to several North Dakota cities and towns. During the 1970s, though, progress on the project slowed. Citizens worried that the project might harm the state's environment. The Canadian government protested the fact that polluted waters might drain into Canada's rivers. In 1986, Congress voted to alter the plan and lessen the possibility of future damage.

Agriculture remains one of the most important industries in North Dakota, and production of crops such as soybeans and sunflowers has been doing well in recent years. The success of agriculture, however, is dependent on weather,

Defending the Nation

In 1957, Minot Air Force Base became a base for missiles and bombers, such as B-52s. In the same year, Grand Forks Air Force base began operations as part of the nation's air defense.

Helping the Herds

Huge herds of bison were reduced to fewer than six hundred animals after the arrival of the white settlers. Because of conservation efforts begun by President Roosevelt and continued to this day, there are about ninety thousand bison in North Dakota.

disease, and consumer demand. In 1997, after a winter of record snowfall, the Red River overflowed, causing the worst flood in state history. In some places, such as Grand Forks, the water rose more than 50 feet (15 m). North Dakotans rolled up their sleeves and went to work, piling sandbags to stop the flow. Floods again struck in 2011, but people were prepared. In 2014, a disease seriously damaged the state's winter wheat crop, and farmers agreed to develop solutions together to prevent the disease from striking again.

The biggest impact on the state in recent decades has been oil drilling. Oil was first discovered on a Williston farm in 1951. More oil wells quickly sprang up. In the 1980s, a new method of oil drilling, **hydraulic fracturing**, or fracking, was developed. This was the start of a new era for many in North Dakota. By June 2014, North Dakota oil wells were producing more than one million barrels per day, turning many wheat farmers into millionaires overnight. An oil boom, like agriculture, is not a sure-fire path to riches, however. There are many problems to face, but North Dakotans have long proven that they can overcome the challenges that come their way.

10 KEY DATES IN STATE HISTORY

1. **1600s**

Several Native American groups, including Dakota, Lakota, Nakota, Hidatsa, Arikara, and Mandan tribes, share the land that is now North Dakota.

2. **December 30, 1803**

The Louisiana Purchase transfers the Missouri River basin of North Dakota from France to the United States.

3. **October 14, 1804**

Captains Meriwether Lewis and William Clark and the Corps of Discovery enter North Dakota. In November, they build a fort along the Knife River.

4. **1812**

North Dakota's first permanent white settlement, made by Irish and Scottish settlers, is established on the site of the Northwest Company's first fur-trading post along the Red River in Pembina.

5. **April 12, 1870**

The Mandan, Hidatsa, and Arikara tribes lose 4 million acres (1.6 million ha) when a presidential executive order creates the 8-million-acre (3.2-million ha) Fort Berthold Reservation.

6. **November 2, 1889**

President Benjamin Harrison approves the admission of North Dakota as the thirty-ninth state in the Union. Republican John Miller is elected the first governor.

7. **April 4, 1951**

The first oil well in the Bakken oil fields begins producing what would be more than twenty-six thousand barrels in its first year.

8. **April-May 1997**

The Red River rises 54 feet (16 m), breaks levees, and floods Fargo and Grand Forks, causing $3.5 billion worth of damage.

9. **October 4-5, 2013**

A surprise blizzard devastates southern and central North Dakota, causing widespread power outages and killing tens of thousands of livestock. President Barack Obama declares a federal disaster.

10. **2015**

Oil prices drop by 50 percent, slowing North Dakota's oil boom, but the state continues to lead the nation in low unemployment, jobs creation, and population growth.

Dancers at Norsk Hostfest are descendants of the Norwegians who helped settle North Dakota.

The People

N orth Dakota prides itself on its close-knit communities. The isolation of the prairie tends to bring people together. The state is the third-least-populous state. It has the second-lowest population density, having slightly less than ten persons per square mile (four persons per sq km) compared to the US average of eighty-seven persons per square mile (thirty-four persons per sq km). As the state has moved into the twenty-first century, citizens face many new issues—loss of farms, the oil boom, and a shift from country living to urban life. Despite changes, challenge is nothing new to North Dakotans. They have survived droughts, floods, and blizzards. As one resident said, "To live here, you've got to be tough."

Heritage

According to the US census in 2010, about 90 percent of the people in North Dakota trace their roots to northern Europe, and today, immigrants from European countries continue to arrive. People of German descent make up 47 percent of the white population, and are the largest ethnic group in the state. Many other North Dakotans trace their roots to Scandinavian countries. In the late 1800s, more than a million people left Norway, and many of them settled in North Dakota. People of Norwegian ancestry make up 30 percent

Who North Dakotans Are

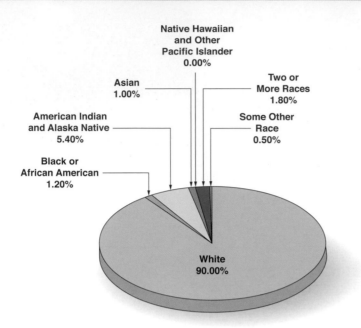

Native Hawaiian and Other Pacific Islander
0.00%

Asian
1.00%

Two or More Races
1.80%

American Indian and Alaska Native
5.40%

Some Other Race
0.50%

Black or African American
1.20%

White
90.00%

Total Population
672,591

Hispanic or Latino (of any race):
• **13,467 people (2%)**

Note: The pie chart shows the racial breakdown of the state's population based on the categories used by the US Bureau of the Census. The Census Bureau reports information for Hispanics or Latinos separately, since they may be of any race. Percentages in the pie chart may not add to 100 because of rounding.

Source: US Bureau of the Census, 2010 Census

of the white population. Immigrants from Sweden, Denmark, and Finland shared many traditions and lifestyles with the Norwegians, and so they easily blended in with the society that was developing in the early days of the state. People from Iceland also moved to the area in the late nineteenth century and settled near the Pembina Escarpment, where the hills and mountains reminded them of home. Today, there are several festivals honoring northern European heritage. Celebrations around the state of traditional arts, food, dance, costumes, and music attract thousands of visitors throughout the year.

Other races and ethnicities are represented in North Dakota, but in smaller numbers. About 1.5 percent of the population is African American. Many are active in the state's communities and government. The same can be said for the Hispanic people in North Dakota. At the last US census, about 2 percent of the population identified themselves as Hispanic, but since then, the Hispanic population has risen higher as people of Hispanic background have come to work on ranches and farms, and in the oil, professional, manufacturing, and service industries. Asians, Asian Americans, Pacific Islanders, and others account for a little more than 1.5 percent of the population. Many newcomers first arrive to live and work in North Dakota's cities, but some prefer a more rural lifestyle.

For the most part, the state has responded positively to its immigrant populations. The government has set up information centers and hotlines that help newcomers solve legal

Residents of Arnegard show their small-town spirit by riding in an Independence Day parade.

issues, obtain citizenship, and understand state laws. City officials have appointed officers who work specifically with immigrant communities.

No matter where they come from, many of these newcomers from different backgrounds continue to honor their native cultures while also embracing American and/or North Dakotan traditions and ways of life. The state government has also approved more money to develop programs and activities that celebrate the state's blend of cultures. Churches, too, play an important role in greeting newcomers and helping them get settled in their new homes.

Native North Dakota

The first people to populate the region that included North Dakota were Native Americans. Today, Native Americans make up about 5.5 percent of the state's population. North Dakota takes its Native American tradition seriously and celebrates it with pride. The Mandan, Hidatsa, Arikara, Yanktonai, Sisseton, Wahpeton, and Hunkpapa (the last four are divisions of the larger group known as the Lakota, or Sioux) along with the Pembina Chippewa and Cree people all add to the state's rich cultural heritage.

North Dakota's Native Americans live across the state in cities and in small towns. Many also live on the state's five major reservations. Many cattle ranching and farming

Phil Jackson

Chuck Klosterman

Peggy Lee

1. John Grass

This member of the Sihasapa Sioux tribe served as the chief justice of the Court of Indian Offenses at the Standing Rock Reservation for forty-two years. He was a peace negotiator and translator between Plains tribes. In 1888, he led resistance toward US government efforts to take more Lakota land.

2. Phil Jackson

Born in 1945, Jackson attended Williston High School. After playing basketball for the New York Knicks, he went on to win eleven NBA championships with the Chicago Bulls and Los Angeles Lakers as head coach.

3. Chuck Klosterman

Chuck Klosterman grew up on a farm in Wyndmere. As a journalist, he has written for the *New York Times*, ESPN, *Washington Post*, and *GQ*. He has also written books, including a memoir of the rock music scene in Fargo.

4. Louis L'Amour

Louis L'Amour, born in Jamestown, traveled the West and wrote more than one hundred Western novels and four hundred short stories, selling millions of copies. Several became movies, such as *How the West Was Won*. He was awarded a Congressional Medal of Honor.

5. Peggy Lee

Peggy Lee, born in Jamestown in 1920, became one of the leading pop and jazz entertainers of her generation. Lee was a songwriter, an actress, and had more than forty hit singles.

6. Kellan Lutz

Actor Kellan Lutz was born in Dickinson in 1985. A TV and movie actor, he has played the role of Emmett Cullen in the Twilight Saga series.

7. Roger Maris

Roger Maris was a baseball outfielder, primarily for the New York Yankees. In 1961, the Fargo native set the record for the most home runs in a single season with sixty-one—a record that stood for almost forty years.

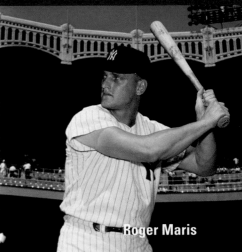

Roger Maris

8. James Rosenquist

Artist James Rosenquist of Grand Forks is a leader of the pop art movement. His work is shown at the Metropolitan Museum of Art and the Whitney and Guggenheim Museums in New York; at the Smithsonian in Washington, DC; and in Paris, London, and Berlin.

9. Eric Sevareid

Eric Sevareid grew up in Minot and was a World War II correspondent. He reported on Paris's surrender to Germany. On assignment to Burma (now Myanmar), his plane was shot down. He was rescued behind enemy lines. He became a commentator for the CBS *Nightly News*.

James Rosenquist

10. Mary Louise Defender Wilson

Defender Wilson, born in 1930, is a Dakota and Hidatsa storyteller who received the 2015 United States Artists fellowship, an honor never before given to a storyteller. Growing up on the Standing Rock Reservation, she learned stories from her grandfather.

Defender Wilson

enterprises, as well as manufacturing and service businesses, are Native American. Tribe-owned businesses, such as casinos, lodges, and tourist attractions are vital parts of the economy of the reservations. The income from these businesses goes toward operating and maintaining the reservations, including funding police and fire departments, and toward providing health care and education for Native Americans. Most of the reservations have their own community colleges, libraries, and technical schools.

Living Languages

North Dakota is also the site of a push to protect and restore Native American languages. Long before European settlers arrived with their own languages, a wealth of Native languages, belonging to more than twenty language families, were spoken in North America.

After the settlers arrived, the population of the Mandan, Hidatsa, and Arikara tribes had fallen so drastically that the three tribes chose to form a single nation, known as the Three Affiliated Tribes. Their Native languages did not belong to the same language families, however. The Hidatsa did not speak a dialect of Lakota, but rather Caddoan. As it was, the Three Affiliated Tribes could not speak each other's languages. After time together, they began to adjust and understand some of what was spoken, but they could not read, write, or speak the other's language. Their solution was to communicate with each other in English, and as the elderly Native speakers passed on, their Native languages were quickly becoming forgotten. Even the Lakota, a much larger group of people, have concerns about the struggle to keep their language alive. Tribal leaders now seek to preserve their spoken and written languages. Linguists, or people who study languages, have joined forces with educators in North and South Dakota to help preserve the Lakota language. This is the language of the nation that once dominated vast stretches of the Great Plains.

In the late 1800s and early 1900s, the government discouraged the use of Lakota. In government-run boarding schools, Native American students caught speaking their Native language were punished. This pattern mostly ended by the 1930s, but by then the damage had been done. The Lakota language was used less frequently. Not until the Lakota gained control of their reservation schools in the 1970s were attempts made to revive the language. However, there was little money available to train teachers or to set up organized ways to teach younger generations the language.

Under a group called the Lakota Language Consortium, educators set up a plan to rewrite the curricula of the school districts that teach large populations of Lakota children.

Doug Parks, assistant director of the American Indian Institute, pointed out that most school curricula are written with white, middle-class students in mind. "There is just no way that Lakota students who live in isolated conditions on a reservation can relate to that," he said.

In 2008 and 2011, the Lakota Language Consortium published dictionaries in the Lakota language. Also in 2011, the group translated twenty episodes of a children's cartoon into Lakota, and the episodes were shown on public television in North and South Dakota. This was the first time an animated cartoon had been shown entirely in a Native American language.

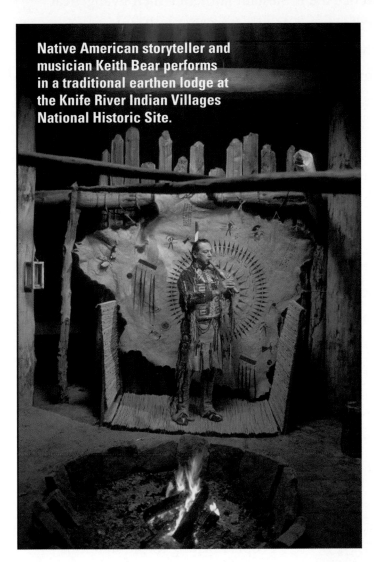

Native American storyteller and musician Keith Bear performs in a traditional earthen lodge at the Knife River Indian Villages National Historic Site.

Education

The very first school in North Dakota was established in 1818 by two French Canadian priests in Pembina. Most early settlements held classes in homes, and many students were homeschooled by parents. North Dakota today has 243 school districts, many of them in very small communities. One of the students' most challenging school experiences is the bus ride to school. Many families live on farms great distances from each other, and in many cases, students can spend an hour or more each way on the school bus. Some buses drive as much as 500 miles (800 km) each day.

There are eleven public colleges and universities in North Dakota. The largest are North Dakota State University and the University of North Dakota. The University of North Dakota is located in Grand Forks and is the oldest school of higher education in the state. It has the only law and medical schools and is known for its school of aeronautical science. North Dakota State University was established in 1890 as an agricultural school. There are five tribal colleges and four private colleges.

Religion

Most of the people of North Dakota practice the Protestant faith, of which Evangelical Lutheran is the largest sect, followed by the United Methodist Church. People who are of the Roman Catholic faith belong to the largest single faith tradition. Other religions include Judaism, Mormonism, and Islam. In the early 1900s, many Lebanese and Syrian farmers immigrated to the northern Great Plains. The very first mosque constructed in the United States was built in the small town of Ross, North Dakota, in 1929. Many North Dakotans attend religious services, and there are more churches per capita in the state than in any other state. Many Native Americans practice traditional rituals and ceremonies, which vary from group to group. Some Native Americans also practice Christianity.

Oil Boom

Just a few years ago, North Dakota's population was dropping and state officials struggled to find ways to keep young people in the state. Then, in 2008, workers began extracting oil from the Bakken Formation, a rock formation beneath land in North Dakota, Montana, and parts of Canada. The oil boom has meant many changes for the state, both good and bad. In many areas, the population has grown very quickly as workers from across the country come to North Dakota for jobs. The state government has made a lot of money, and as of late 2015, North Dakota had the lowest unemployment rate in the United States. However, the oil boom has also put a strain on sewage systems, roads, and water supplies.

Oil wells are sprouting like grain on the Bakken Formation, bringing a rush of workers into the state.

People flocking to the state can be a boon to businesses as well as to government and overall citizen welfare. However, the increase in the number of people moving to the small towns where oil is being produced is creating many shortages. Housing has become extremely expensive and hard to come by. Rental housing and real estate costs are easily some of the highest in the nation, and many new arrivals can't afford a house. Many people find themselves living in trailers or temporary camps. Schools are also hard

Farming and ranching have been on the decline in North Dakota.

pressed to accommodate all the incoming students. Classrooms are full, and many of them are in modular buildings. There is also a shortage of teachers.

City and Country

Farming has been a long and proud tradition in the Peace Garden State. In recent years, however, North Dakota's farmers have been facing new and greater struggles. Farming technology has replaced many of the jobs once done by farm workers, and in order to compete and be as efficient as possible, farmers must invest in the technology, which can be extremely expensive. Recent unpredictable weather events such as blizzards, floods, and drought have damaged livestock herds and reduced crop yields. Some farmers have been forced to sell or lease their land and move to cities to find other work.

North Dakota's cities are growing. Several national companies employ North Dakotans. There are theaters, restaurants, concerts, and sporting events, as well as numerous museums, several devoted to Western art, Native American art, and Great Plains history. Living off the land has been a way of life for Native Americans and the farmers and ranchers who came to the state later. Now oil production is making cities out of towns, and the original cities, and their suburban neighborhoods, are growing and thriving. North Dakotans have many new choices and a wealth of tradition to guide them.

Fort Union Trading Post Rendezvous

Killdeer Mountain Roundup Rodeo

1. Central North Dakota Steam Thresher's Reunion

This is one of New Rockford's biggest annual events. It is held the third weekend of September and features a variety of antique farm machinery, tractor rides, dancing, and craft shows.

2. Fort Union Trading Post Rendezvous

The Fort Union Trading Post Rendezvous features replicas of Native American encampments and fur-trading posts. Visitors enjoy campfires, fiddle music, and demonstrations of traditional skills.

3. German Folk Festival

People come to Fargo from all over each July to celebrate the area's German heritage with music, costumes, and food. In addition to booths with arts and crafts, special performances are scheduled, such as a forty-five-piece youth band from Germany.

4. Great Tomato Festival

This fun event, held in August, features a silent auction, live music, and a menu full of tomato-based treats. The money raised benefits community organizations in Minot, such as the public library, art museums, and the symphony orchestra.

5. Killdeer Mountain Roundup Rodeo

The Killdeer Mountain rodeo is the state's oldest. In July, people cheer on daring displays of bull riding, roping, and barrel racing. Young people from "age zero" to fourteen compete in pole bending, goat tail tying, and in horse, calf, sheep, and steer riding events

★ NORTH DAKOTA ★

6. Norsk Hostfest

This October event is the largest Scandanavian festival in North America, featuring the culture of five Nordic countries. Held in Minot, the event attracts tens of thousands. Highlights include music and dance performances, and traditional crafts and foods.

7. North Dakota State Fair

The state fair is held every July, featuring carnival rides, concerts, agricultural exhibits, livestock competitions, pet shows, games, food, music, and arts and crafts. Contestants also vie for prizes in writing, cooking, photography, and quilt-making.

8. Ryan Keplin Summer Fest

The Ryan Keplin Summer Fest in Rollette is a celebration of the culture of the Métis—people of mixed French and Native American heritage. Visitors enjoy country and fiddle music; clogging, jigging, and square dancing; and foods and crafts.

9. Tri-County Fair

Since 1927, the Tri-County Fair in Wishek has entertained fairgoers with stock car races, demolition derbies, antique and custom car shows, livestock and pet shows, rodeos, and carnival rides. People also enjoy food, concerts, and arts and crafts.

10. United Tribes Powwow

More than fifteen hundred Native Americans from seventy tribes gather at the United Tribes Technical College in Bismarck for one of the country's largest powwows. Dancers and drummers compete, and guests enjoy games, races, parades, foods, and music.

Norsk Hostfest

North Dakota State Fair

The people of North Dakota were divided in their opinion over the nickname for the state university's sports teams.

How the Government Works

4

North Dakotans want a bright future for their state. They look to their leaders to make strong choices and decisions that will benefit all. The state's politicians deal with many important concerns, and to come to the best decisions, they debate and compromise. The process of government is open to everyone, however. New laws or policies are often suggested by voters. Many citizens have good ideas about how their state could be better run. In North Dakota, it is important that many voices are heard. After all, new laws and policies affect the lives of everyone.

North Dakotans serve their local governments in countless ways. They often act as lawmakers and managers and make decisions that influence local lives. The state currently has nearly four hundred towns and cities. Each of these local units chooses how they want their community to be run. The daily affairs of the city may be overseen by a mayor, a council, a manager, or a board of commissioners. These leaders make sure that roads are safe and citizens have access to government-run services and programs.

The county is another level of local government. North Dakota is divided into fifty-three counties. Each county is run by a board of commissioners. The boards have three to five members who serve terms of four years. Board members are responsible for most aspects of county business. They must ensure that all of the county's communities are equally served. Financial planners, sheriffs, school superintendents, and state attorneys are just some of the people who play a vital role in the life of North Dakota's counties.

State officials have the hard job of running the state as a whole. They collect and spend the state's funds on a variety of programs and projects. Some of the areas on which officials focus are Native American affairs, agriculture, tourism, wildlife, and the arts. Some state leaders manage highway safety, while others work on bringing new companies and more businesses to the state. There are many jobs to be done in a state in which citizens have a wide range of needs and concerns.

Branches of Government

As in most states, there are three branches in North Dakota's government.

Executive

The governor heads the executive branch. He or she helps create the state budget and makes sure the state's business runs smoothly. Other officials of the executive branch—the lieutenant governor; secretary of state; attorney general; treasurer; auditor; and tax, insurance, agriculture, and public service commissioners, as well as the superintendent of public instruction—are elected by the state's voters. These officials serve four-year terms.

Legislative

The state's legislative assembly is divided into two parts. The senate has forty-seven members. The house of representatives is made up of ninety-four elected officials. Together, the members help to make the laws that all North Dakotans must follow. Many of these legislators, or lawmakers, also serve on committees. They focus on issues that are important to the state such as agriculture, transportation, and education.

Silly Law

Fireworks are legal on Independence Day and New Year's Eve in many communities. However, on New Year's Eve in Devil's Lake, fireworks can only be set off between 8:00 a.m. and 11:00 p.m., missing midnight celebrations by an hour.

Judicial

The North Dakota judicial system consists of the supreme court, the court of appeals, district courts, and municipal courts. The North Dakota Supreme Court is the highest court in the state. It is made up of five justices, or judges. They are elected for ten-year terms. One of the

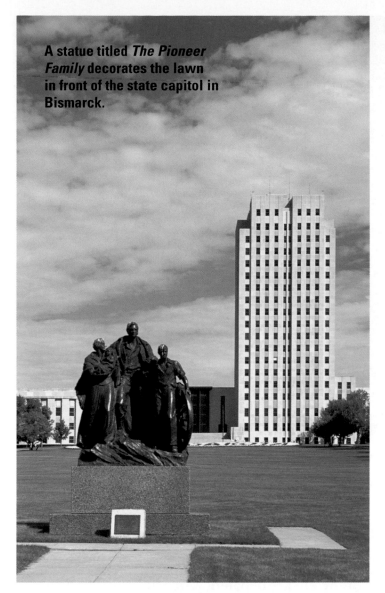
A statue titled *The Pioneer Family* decorates the lawn in front of the state capitol in Bismarck.

five is the chief justice, chosen by the supreme court and district court justices. He or she presides over court conferences, administrates the court's activities, and represents the judicial system to the people. The supreme court oversees the decisions made by lower courts, ensuring that they are fair and that the laws of the state constitution are being upheld.

The court of appeals hears cases that are assigned to it by the supreme court. The three justices of the court of appeals hear cases brought by people who are unhappy with a lower court ruling. There are seven judicial districts in North Dakota, and these courts hear cases that lower courts are unable to decide. District courts hear criminal and misdemeanor cases, and they preside over juvenile court, family court, and civil court. Municipal courts are city courts that preside over the breaking of laws enacted by the city, such as disturbing the peace or parking illegally.

From Bill to Law

The process by which a bill becomes a law often involves many steps. When a citizen or legislator has an idea for a law, it must be proposed in written form. A group called the Legislative Management then gives the bill an official number and has it printed so that every legislator can read what is being proposed. The bill's title is then read by the secretary of the senate or the chief clerk of the house of representatives, depending on which house is introducing the bill. This is known as the first reading.

The North Dakota house of representatives debates and votes on laws in this chamber.

Next, the bill is open for discussion and debate. It is then referred, or sent, to what is called a standing committee. The state has several standing committees. Each group focuses on a particular topic or issue. A bill about fishing licenses, for example, would be sent to the Natural Resources Committee. The assigned committee then holds a public hearing. The state's citizens are welcome to attend these important meetings and express their views. This is when certain points of the bill are debated. After the committee has looked into all parts of the bill, it reports back to the other members in the house.

In Their Own Words

"If it had not been for what I learned during the years I spent in North Dakota, I never in the world would have been president of the United States."
—President Theodore Roosevelt

The members either pass, do not pass, amend (change) the bill, or refer it to another committee that will look into it in more depth.

The chamber of the legislature that first proposed the bill then votes on it. If the members are in favor of the bill, it moves on to the other half of the state's legislature, either the senate or the house of representatives. Once there, the bill goes through a similar process. A committee examines and discusses it. Often it makes changes or suggestions. If that happens, the bill has to be approved by both parts of the legislature again. If each house agrees, the bill is then signed by the leader of the senate and the house of representatives. It is then sent to the governor.

The governor can either approve or veto (reject) the bill. If he or she vetoes it, the bill is sent back to the legislature. Two-thirds of the members of both the senate and the house of representatives must vote in favor of the bill if it then is to become a law. Once a bill is approved, it is sent to the secretary of state and made official. In North Dakota, most new laws take effect on August 1 of each year.

Righting a Wrong

Prior to 1924, Native Americans could not vote in local, state, and federal elections, unless they had left their tribe. However, after many Native Americans fought in World War I, Congress passed the "Indian Freedom Citizenship Suffrage Act of 1924," granting Native Americans citizenship and the right to vote.

Tribal Government

The Native Americans of North Dakota have tribal governments within their reservations. Each has a constitution that sets the laws for their individual tribe. At the head of tribal government is an elected council, which is led by a chairperson. All council members must reside in their districts and must be enrolled members of the tribe. The reservations have jurisdiction over their reservation land and airspace, as well as mineral and water rights. Tribal governments also work with the state of North Dakota in an official group called the North Dakota Indian Affairs Commission. The state governor leads the commission and appoints three members, two of which must be Native American. The chairpersons of each tribal council are also members of the commission. Together, they work to improve the standard of living for people on the reservations and to encourage Native American involvement in local and statewide businesses and government.

POLITICAL FIGURES
FROM NORTH DAKOTA

Dick Armey: US Congressman, 1985-2003

The conservative Dick Armey was born in Cando and graduated from Jamestown College and the University of North Dakota. After teaching economics at two universities in Texas, he was elected to congress in that state. He served as house majority leader from 1995 to 2003. He sponsored the bill that created the Department of Homeland Security.

Warren Christopher: US Secretary of State, 1993-1997

Born in Scranton in 1925, Warren Christopher was the US deputy secretary of state from 1977 to 1981, when he helped secure the release of fifty-two American hostages held in Iran. In 1993, Christopher was sworn in as the sixty-third US secretary of state. He helped negotiate the Oslo Accords between Israel and the Palestinians.

Heidi Heitkamp: US Senator, 2013-

Mary Kathryn Heitkamp grew up in Mantador, North Dakota. A graduate of the University of North Dakota and Lewis and Clark College, she was an attorney for the US Environmental Protection Agency. She serves on many Senate committees including Agriculture, Homeland Security, and Indian Affairs.

NORTH DAKOTA
YOU CAN MAKE A DIFFERENCE

Contacting Lawmakers

North Dakota has two US senators, as all states do, and one member in the US House of Representatives. To contact them, visit:

www.govtrack.us/congress/members/ND

Click on the person's name and then on the contact link to reach your elected official.

If you are interested in contacting North Dakota's state legislators, go to

www.legis.nd.gov

Scroll to the bottom and select "Find My Legislator". Then enter your house number and zip code to access a legislator's contact information and biography.

Fighting for a Cause

In 2000, Native Americans and concerned citizens sent petitions to the state legislature requesting that the University of North Dakota stop using the nickname "Fighting Sioux," and to discontinue using a logo showing a Lakota (Sioux) warrior wearing a feathered headband. A bill was proposed but died in committee. In 2005, the National Collegiate Athletic Association (NCAA) determined that all schools must remove nicknames and logos referring to Native Americans. The NCAA made an exception for any school whose area tribe permitted the use. The Spirit Lake Lakota tribe gave permission, but not the Standing Rock Lakota tribe. The legislature responded to citizens' requests and removed the name.

In 2009, however, other citizens who wanted to restore the name and logo sent letters and petitions to the legislature, which passed a law reinstating the nickname and logo and insisted the university use them. Citizens finally demanded a statewide election to determine the fate of the nickname and logo as everyone agreed the issue should be settled by the people. In June 2012, a large majority voted to remove the nickname and logo from the school. On November 18, 2015, the University of North Dakota announced its new nickname: "The Fighting Hawks." While there was much back and forth in this debate, both tribal and non-tribal citizens and their state government worked together for a resolution.

ROWNING'S HONEY
HO FALLS ID J
0-529-3692 7

North Dakota is one of the leading states for producing honey.

Making a Living

North Dakota is farm country. Agriculture helped to build the state and make it strong. Though the farm industry is starting to decline, it continues to be a major source of the state's income. Residents and government officials have long supported laws and programs that would help the state's farmers. Powerful political groups such as the Nonpartisan League (NPL) forever changed the way the state does business. In the 1910s and 1920s, the NPL pushed a series of reforms that helped ease the farmer's way of life, such as lower taxes, crop insurance, and favorable bank loans. North Dakota is the only state in the nation that has a state bank, providing personalized financial services to its citizens. It also has a state-run grain mill and storage facility. To this day, in the minds of many North Dakotans, farmers and ranchers come first.

In 1957, the Economic Development Commission was created to attract businesses to the state. The idea caught on, and now more than eighty communities have similar groups. As time goes on, the state has also looked for other ways of earning money. While farming will continue to be important to the state's economy, leaders are searching for new ways, such as oil production and manufacturing, to keep the state thriving in the twenty-first century.

Agriculture

North Dakota's economy cannot be examined without taking a look at agriculture. Much of the state's wealth is locked in its soil. Almost 90 percent of the state's land is devoted to farming and ranching. According to the 2012 US agricultural census, there are about thirty-one thousand farms in the state, producing nearly $11 billion worth of food and other products, such as wool and landscape plants. The state is a top producer of barley, durum spring wheat, all types of dry edible beans, dry peas, oats, sunflowers, canola, and flaxseed. Most of the state's high-quality durum wheat goes into almost all of the pasta that is consumed by Americans. It ranks second in the production of navy beans and pinto beans. North Dakota is one of four states that produce most of the nation's potatoes, sugar beets, and honey.

Barley is grown mostly in eastern North Dakota, while the bright, bobbing faces of sunflowers blanket the Drift Prairie region. North Dakota grows more sunflowers than any other state. Most of the sunflowers are grown as a snack food, and nearly half of the crop is exported. Corn is plentiful along the southern plains. The corn helps feed the state's hogs. Grass thrives across the state as well. It is cut, dried, and gathered into bales or piles. The hay is then used mostly to feed North Dakota's large herds of cattle.

An abundance of wheat is grown on a farm south of Binford, in Griggs County.

North Dakota's great grazing lands allow cattle to prosper and contribute to the state's economy.

Livestock is another major part of the state's economy. The vast grasslands of central and western North Dakota offer the ideal place for cattle to roam and graze. There are about 1.8 million head of cattle in the state. They are raised not only for their meat. Dairy farms dot the southern plains. Nearly six hundred farms raise chickens, some for food and others for eggs. Hogs are raised mostly on smaller farms in the south and southeast. Some North Dakota ranchers raise sheep, donkeys, and horses.

Like other midwestern farm economies, the state has had a gradual decline in farming through the years. The number of farms today is about half the number that existed in the 1950s. This decrease in the number of farms has not delivered a major blow to North Dakota's economy, though. While there are fewer farms overall, farm size has increased. Improved machinery means smaller operations can successfully farm more land.

Mining

North Dakota land is rich in many minerals. It has major deposits of lignite coal. Lignite coal, also called brown coal, is used as a fuel source. Officials estimate that 400 to 600 billion tons (363 billion to 544 billion metric tons) of lignite coal lie beneath western North Dakota. The southwest is rich in various types of clay used for pottery and brick-

1. Alternative Energy

North Dakota is developing alternative energy—power from solar, ethanol, and gas from methane produced by cows. Farmers install solar panels to power water pumps in remote areas. Wind farms across the open plains currently produce electricity for 420,000 homes.

2. Aviation Manufacturing

Given that there are two US Air Force bases in North Dakota, the manufacture of aviation products, including unmanned aircraft, or drones, is an important industry. North Dakota is one of six national safety test sites for unmanned aircraft.

3. Farm Machinery

Farms are important to the economy, and the state has many factories that manufacture farm equipment. Some large plants are based in Fargo and Bismarck, while smaller operations can be found in Wahpeton, Minot, and Pembina.

4. Food Processing

North Dakota processes most of the food products produced in the state. There are grain mills and meat packing factories. Many processors press crops into cooking oils such as canola, corn, sunflower, and soybean. Sugar beets are processed into cane sugar.

5. Honey

North Dakota is the nation's leading honey producer, with bees producing almost 35 million pounds (15.8 million kg) each year. The pure honey is sold nationwide. It is also combined with other foods in the state's food processing plants.

Aviation Manufacturing

Farm Machinery

NORTH DAKOTA

6. Oil

Oil is the second-largest industry in the state, and North Dakota is the second-largest oil-producing state in the country. As of 2016, there were more than thirteen thousand oil wells in the state, and more were being built.

7. Sunflowers

North Dakota grows more sunflowers than any other state, about half the country's crop. They are sold as flowers, or their seeds are used as snacks and for making cooking oil. The seeds are sold in the United States and exported to Europe.

8. Technology

In 2015, more than 3,280 businesses employed North Dakotans in various technology fields, including information technology, component manufacturing, finance, and marketing. The country's second-largest Microsoft campus is in Fargo. Other technology companies include Hitachi, Amazon, and Unisys.

9. Tourism

Tourism is North Dakota's third-leading source of income, adding around $3 billion to the state's economy each year. People come to see the badlands, the International Peace Garden, or to enjoy the wide open spaces.

10. Wheat

North Dakota is one of the country's top wheat-producing states, often trading off for the top spot with Kansas. For many years, countries around the world have imported different types of wheat from North Dakota. These types of wheat include hard red spring and durum.

Oil

Wheat

Recipe for Honey Sunflower Seed Energy Bars

Make and enjoy a tasty and very healthy treat, complements of North Dakota farmers.

What You Need

2 mixing bowls; one must be glass (microwavable)

Mixing spoon

8 by 8 inch (20 by 20 cm) baking dish

Measuring cups and spoons

1 teaspoon (5 milliliters) vegetable oil

1½ cups (355 mL) rolled oats

½ cup (119 mL) unsweetened raisins

½ cup (119 mL) shelled sunflower seeds

1 teaspoon (5 mL) cinnamon

¼ cup (59 mL) sunflower seed butter, or other nut/seed butter, such as peanut butter

⅓ cup (78 mL) honey

1 teaspoon (5 mL) vanilla extract

3 tablespoons (44 mL) chocolate chips (optional)

½ cup (119 mL) dry shredded coconut (optional)

What To Do

- Preheat oven to 350°F (177°C).
- Coat baking dish with oil or cooking spray.
- In a bowl, mix the oats, raisins, sunflower seeds, coconut, and cinnamon. Set aside.
- In a microwaveable bowl, stir the honey, vanilla, and sunflower seed butter or peanut butter.
- Microwave for 30 to 60 seconds, until combined and pourable.
- Pour honey mixture over oats and stir.
- Scoop into baking dish.
- Wet hands slightly and press down on mixture to spread evenly. Sprinkle with chocolate chips if desired.
- Bake for 15 minutes, until golden brown.
- Allow to cool completely before slicing into bars.

making. Sand and gravel are important products found across the entire state. They are used mainly for building roads.

Oil and Natural Gas

When oil was discovered near Tioga in 1951, it became North Dakota's most valuable mined product. Slowly the oil industry developed in the state, and by 1970, there were oil wells in fourteen western North Dakota counties. Today, North Dakota is the second largest oil-producing state, and workers are drilling for more and more oil every day. In November 2015, 1.1 million barrels of oil were produced daily.

According to government scientists, the Bakken Formation has the largest deposit of oil and natural gas in the United States outside of Alaska. Though the formation has been mined since 1955, a new method of drilling, called hydraulic fracturing, or "fracking," has turned parts of North Dakota into a hub for national energy production. The fracking process begins by drilling a deep shaft, then turning sideways and drilling horizontally. Pressurized torrents of water, sand, and chemicals break up the rock, called shale, releasing oil and natural gas.

Oil production is bringing billions of dollars each year to the state. What this means for rural communities around the Bakken, such as Williston and the Fort Berthold Reservation, is extraordinary wealth. These communities are benefiting from jobs—in construction, retail, education, healthcare, manufacturing, and services. The income is going into new schools, recreation centers, improved roads, shopping, entertainment, and better-quality health care. There are about 1,300 oil wells on the Fort Berthold Reservation, and in 2014, the Three Affiliated Tribes drilled four wells of their own.

In Their Own Words

"This oil boom is just wild and crazy. It's more than you can fathom."
—Ward Koeser, recently retired mayor of Williston

Although people living near the Bakken oil fields and others statewide are benefiting financially from drilling, everyone knows there are environmental risks to producing oil and natural gas. Fracking requires large amounts of water, sand, and chemicals. Although the water mixture is reused, it eventually becomes too full of toxic chemicals and must be trucked to wastewater treatment plants or storage containers. There is always danger that the chemicals can leak into and poison the water supply. Heavy trucks, trains, and pipelines transport the oil and natural gas from the oil fields. Accidents happen and oil spills result, contaminating the soil. Chemical fumes from drilling cause air pollution and smog. The US Environmental Protection Agency is enacting strict regulations for oil producers to follow.

A welder works on a tractor at a factory in Fargo.

Manufacturing

With so many crops being grown in the Peace Garden State, cities such as Fargo, Grand Forks, Minot, and Bismarck have many food processing plants which contribute to the state's income. Factories and business centers in these cities process grain, meat, and dairy products.

The state's many varieties of wheat are turned into pasta and bread. Potatoes are peeled, sliced, and made into enough French fries to supply many fast-food restaurants for a year. Milk is placed in containers and shipped to stores across the area or turned into delicious cheeses. The meat produced in the state becomes steaks and sausages. North Dakota's workers help to keep their state and the nation well fed.

North Dakota factories also produce farm equipment and supplies. Farm-related items are not the only products made. The state's workers also make cabinets and furniture, computer software, construction equipment, and airplane parts.

Retail and Services

The various jobs that make up North Dakota's service industries account for a large part of the state's annual income. These businesses are mostly located in or near the state's urban centers. Grocery stores, restaurants, gas stations, and hardware stores all add their share to North Dakota's earnings. Real estate and tourism are also important to the economy.

Wetlands in Grand Forks County reflect the beautiful skies over North Dakota.

Grand Forks, Bismarck, and Fargo have large medical centers that employ thousands of people. Law firms, banks, insurance companies, and shops that repair cars and farm equipment also contribute to the economy.

Transportation is very important to North Dakota. People need to be able to travel around the large state. The state's valuable farm and mineral products must also be shipped great distances to urban centers. Pipelines carry oil and natural gas, while trucks and trains haul the state's crops and coal. Without these important transportation providers, the state would be unable to cash in on its agricultural and mineral wealth.

The first years of the twenty-first century have brought many changes to North Dakota. From a declining population and devastating floods to a record-breaking oil boom, a growing population, and a budget surplus, the state has seen many highs and lows.

Today, North Dakotans remain dedicated to their state and ready to grow. They still honor the traditions of the past and the ways of life that have guided their state steadily through the years. They also keep their eyes fixed on the future. Making success out of hard times, standing united and proud, North Dakotans know there are few challenges they cannot overcome.

NORTH DAKOTA
STATE MAP

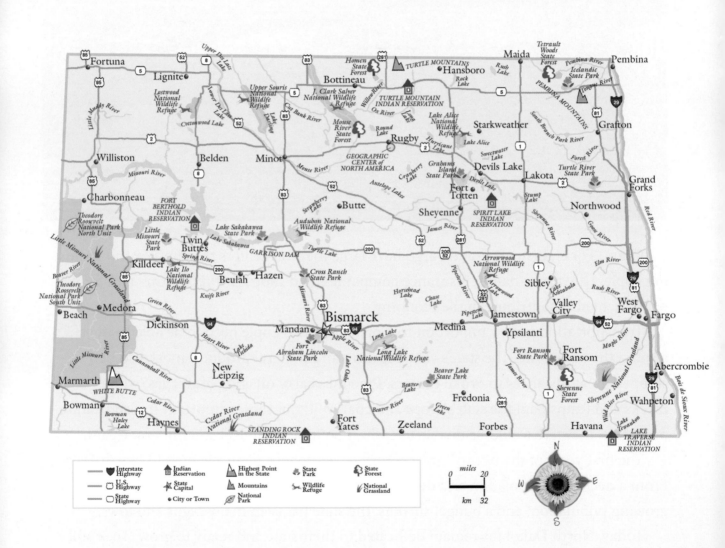

Fortuna • Lignite • Upper Des Lacs Lake • Homen State Forest • Maida • Tetrault Woods State Forest • Pembina River • Icelandic State Park • Pembina

Little Muddy River • Lostwood National Wildlife Refuge • Lower Des Lacs Lake • Cottonwood Lake • Upper Souris National Wildlife Refuge • Lake Darling • Cut Bank River • J. Clark Salyer National Wildlife Refuge • Bottineau • TURTLE MOUNTAINS • Hansboro • Rock Lake • Rush Lake • PEMBINA MOUNTAINS

Williston • Belden • Minot • Mouse River • Willow River • Mouse River State Forest • Round Lake • Ox River • TURTLE MOUNTAIN INDIAN RESERVATION • Lake Alice National Wildlife Refuge • Starkweather • Rugby • Hurricane Lake • Lake Alice • Sweetwater Lake • South Branch Park River • Grafton

Charbonneau • Missouri River • GEOGRAPHIC CENTER of NORTH AMERICA • Cranberry Lake • Grahams Island State Park • Devils Lake • Lakota • Turtle River State Park • Forest River • Goose River • Red River • Grand Forks

Theodore Roosevelt National Park North Unit • FORT BERTHOLD INDIAN RESERVATION • Little Missouri State Park • Antelope Lakes • Fort Totten • Sheyenne • SPIRIT LAKE INDIAN RESERVATION • Stump Lake • Sheyenne River • Northwood

Little Missouri National Grassland • Beaver River • Killdeer • Lake Ilo National Wildlife Refuge • Twin Buttes • Lake Sakakawea State Park • Lake Sakakawea • GARRISON DAM • Strawberry Lake • Turtle Lake • Audubon National Wildlife Refuge • James River • Arrowwood National Wildlife Refuge • Sibley • Lake Ashtabula • Elm River • Rush River

Theodore Roosevelt National Park South Unit • Green River • Beulah • Hazen • Spring River • Knife River • Cross Ranch State Park • Horsehead Lake • Chase Lake • Pipestem Lake • Arrowwood Lake • Valley City • West Fargo

Medora • Beach • Dickinson • Heart River • Lake Tschida • Mandan • Bismarck • Apple River • Long Lake • Medina • Long Lake National Wildlife Refuge • Jamestown • Pipestem Lake • Ypsilanti • Fort Ransom State Park • Fort Ransom • Maple River • Fargo

Marmarth • Cannonball River • WHITE BUTTE • New Leipzig • Fort Abraham Lincoln State Park • Lake Oahe • Beaver Lake State Park • Beaver Lake • James River • Sheyenne State Forest • Wild Rice River • Sheyenne National Grassland • Abercrombie • Bois de Sioux River

Bowman • Cedar River • Heart River • Little Missouri River • Bowman Haley Lake • Cedar River National Grassland • STANDING ROCK INDIAN RESERVATION • Fort Yates • Beaver River • Green Lake • Zeeland • Fredonia • Forbes • Havana • Wahpeton • Lake Traverse • LAKE TRAVERSE INDIAN RESERVATION

Haynes

Legend

- Interstate Highway
- U.S. Highway
- State Highway
- Indian Reservation
- State Capital
- City or Town
- Highest Point in the State
- Mountains
- National Park
- State Park
- Wildlife Refuge
- State Forest
- National Grassland

miles
0   20
km   32

N E S W

NORTH DAKOTA
MAP SKILLS

1. What highway would you take to go to Devil's Lake from Grand Forks?

2. Which Native American reservation is east of Standing Rock Reservation?

3. Which city contains the junction of two US Interstate highways?

4. Is the geographic center of North America north or south of Bismarck?

5. Which city lies on the northern border of Theodore Roosevelt National Park?

6. Which highway and which direction would you take to go from Minot to the state capital?

7. Name five major cities along the Red River, north to south.

8. Which town is closer to the Fort Berthold Reservation: Williston or Fort Yates?

9. Which state park is closer to Mandan: Little Missouri or Fort Abraham Lincoln?

10. Are the Turtle Mountains north, south, east, or west of Lignite?

Devil's Lake in winter

Fort Abraham Lincoln State Park

1. Highway 2
2. Lake Traverse Reservation
3. Fargo
4. North
5. Charbonneau
6. Highway 83 heading south
7. Pembina, Grand Forks, Fargo, Abercrombie, Wahpeton
8. Williston
9. Fort Abraham Lincoln State Park
10. East

State Flag, Seal, and Song

The state seal shows a tree, three bundles of wheat, a plow, an anvil, a hammer, a bow with three arrows, and a Native American hunting a bison at sunset. Above the tree is a half circle with forty-two stars and the motto "Liberty and Union Now and Forever, One and Inseparable." October 1 is to the left of the seal and the year 1889 to the right. Over the seal are the words "Great Seal," and under, "State of North Dakota."

The state flag, adopted in 1911, displays a bald eagle holding an olive branch and a bundle of arrows. In its beak is a ribbon with the Latin words "E Pluribus Unum," meaning "Many unite as one." Thirteen stars, representing the original colonies, appear above the eagle. A shield displays thirteen red and white stripes. "North Dakota" is written below the eagle.

"North Dakota, North Dakota, with thy prairies wide and free," begins the official state song, the "North Dakota Hymn." The lyrics were written by James W. Foley in 1926, put to music by Dr. C. S. Putnam in 1927, and adopted in 1947. Here is the link for the lyrics and sheet music:

ndstudies.gov/state_song

Glossary

badlands — A barren region of heavily eroded, harsh rocky terrain.

confluence — The junction of two rivers, especially rivers of approximately equal width.

dugouts — Small, round dwellings built into hillsides and made of blocks of mud.

endangered — Something that is at risk of dying off.

escarpment — A long, steep slope, usually at the edge of a plateau.

glaciers — Slowly moving masses of ice and rock.

Great Depression — A drastic decline in the world economy resulting in mass unemployment and widespread poverty that lasted from 1929 until 1939.

Hydraulic fracturing — Also called fracking, a drilling method for oil and natural gas that breaks rock using pressurized water, sand, and chemicals.

immunity — The ability of an organism to defend itself from germs using special blood cells and antibodies.

Louisiana Purchase — The territory, including the western part of the Mississippi valley and the present state Louisiana, sold by France to the United States in 1803.

naturalist — A person who is an expert in natural history, plants, or animals.

nomadic — Describing the way of life of people who move from place to place, taking their belongings with them.

reservation — In terms of a Native American reservation, an area of land owned and governed by a tribe or tribes.

reservoir — A large natural or artificial body of water used to store water for future use. Many reservoirs are created by dams.

skirmishes — Irregular or unplanned fighting, especially involving small or outlying parts of armies or navies.

More About North Dakota

BOOKS

Berne, Emma Carlson. *Sacagawea: Crossing the Continent with Lewis & Clark*. Sterling Biographies. New York: Sterling, 2010.

Bjorklund, Ruth. *The Pros and Cons of Natural Gas and Fracking*. The Economics of Energy. New York: Cavendish Square Publishing, 2014.

Gish, Melissa. *Bison*. Living Wild. Mankato, MN: Creative Education, 2012.

Stanley, George Edward. *Sitting Bull: Great Sioux Hero*. Sterling Biographies. New York: Sterling Publishers, 2011.

WEBSITES

National Park Service Theodore Roosevelt National Park, North Dakota
www.nps.gov/thro

North Dakota Tourism
www.ndtourism.com

Official Portal for North Dakota State Government
www.nd.gov

ABOUT THE AUTHORS

Doug Sanders has written several titles in the It's My State! series. In writing this book, he drove across North Dakota, talking to the state's friendly residents. He especially loved hiking in Theodore Roosevelt National Park.

Ruth Bjorklund lives on Bainbridge Island, Washington, with her family. She has written many books for young people and is thankful to have visited every state.

Index

Page numbers in **boldface** are illustrations. Entries in **boldface** are glossary terms.

Index